Native Nations
Intertribal Cookbook

Native Nations Intertribal Cookbook

West and Midwest

Recipes collected from the major tribes of the Midwest and West

Stanley Groves

Thank the Grandfather for the Harvest

Bless the Work of our Hands

Copyright © 2013 by Stanley Groves.

Library of Congress Control Number:		2013901308
ISBN:	Hardcover	978-1-4797-8393-9
	Softcover	978-1-4797-8392-2
	Ebook	978-1-4797-8394-6

All rights reserved. No part of this book may be reproduced or transmitted in any form or by any means, electronic or mechanical, including photocopying, recording, or by any information storage and retrieval system, without permission in writing from the copyright owner.

This book was printed in the United States of America.

To order additional copies of this book, contact:
Xlibris Corporation
1-888-795-4274
www.Xlibris.com
Orders@Xlibris.com
118948

Other Books written:

Native Nations Intertribal Cookbook

Recipes collected from the East Coast

Stanley E. Groves (One Horse)

Published November 2011 by XLIBRIS

ISBN13 Hardcover   978-1-4653-4905-7
ISBN13 Softcover   978-1-4653-4904-0
ISBN13 eB00k   978-1-4653-4904-4

Order from your Local Book Store, Xlibris or Amazon.com

Books to be published:

Native Nations Desserts Cookbook
Native Nations Native Foods Cookbook

        Enjoy the Recipes of all my books

THE ETERNAL FLAME

A flame carried from Cherokee, N.C. to Oklahoma during the Trail of Tears. This Flame is still burning in both places and is cause for us to remember the flame of love not the flame of hate.

I dedicate this collection of recipes to the following people . . .

Paula Groves (my Wife)
Bear Bozarth
Bonnie Lewis
Stephanie Ford
Lucy Crume
And the entire Native People of the U. S. A

May this be a symbol of friendship; Eternal 'Twixt the American Natives and our White Brothers

The recipes that follow are for wild game and plants but may also be used with domesticated meat, poultry, and plants.

The spices and seasonings used in these recipes are mostly modern rather than authentic, but obscure and difficult-to-obtain original ingredients.

Every effort has been made to ensure that the information in this book is complete and accurate.

These recipes are rich in Native American folklore, retaining the quaint mystery which our forbears endowed them. These men and women found fullness of life in the quiet woodlands

of this great country. Let us give gratitude and adoration to the Great Spirit for their contribution.

All of the Native American foods are not by any means contained in this endeavor, but surely some of the best are included. The world would surely be devoid of some of the best food if the Native American way of cooking should suddenly disappear.

All rights reserved. This book, or parts thereof, may not be reproduced in any form without permission of the author.

The cultural differences, linked to distinct geographical locations and regional growing seasons, determined how these various peoples lived, what they ate, and how they cooked. Most of the food prepared was done so salt free as salt was not readily available. Food was spiced to taste according to what was available during the season.

Native American cuisine includes all food practices of the indigenous peoples of the Americas. Information about Native American cuisine comes from a great variety of sources. Modern-day Native peoples retain a rich body of traditional foods, some of which have become iconic of present-day Native American social gatherings (for example, frybread). Foods like cornbread, turkey, cranberry, blueberry, hominy and mush are known to have been adopted into the cuisine of the United States from Native American groups. In other cases, documents from the early periods of contact with European, African, and Asian peoples allow the recovery of food practices which passed out of popularity. Modern-day Native American cuisine can cover as wide of range as the imagination of the chef who adopts or adapts this cuisine to present. The use of indigenous domesticated and wild food ingredients can represent Native American food and cuisine. North American Native Cuisine can differ somewhat from Southwestern and Mexican Cuisine in its simplicity and directness of flavor. The use of ramps, wild ginger, miners' lettuce, and juniper can impart subtle flavors to various dishes.

West of the Mississippi, farmland gave way to the prairies, where the Plains Indians followed the great buffalo, turning it into food, clothing, tools and shelter. For the most part the land was fertile enough to farm not all tribes followed the buffalo like the Siouan tribes, the Osage, Mandan, Kiowa, and others led a more settled life centered around crops of corn, beans, squash (the three sisters) and tomatoes.

Indian cooking of the Southwest is varied and colorful as the land that produces it. This is the country of pinon, ponderosa pine and cactus. At meals there might have been squash blossoms fried to a golden crispness, pinon soup, adobe bread and a crisp salad of marinated cucumbers.

Tribes of the Northwest Coast lived from the sea, and they lived richly. The Pacific served up whale, halibut, flounder, herring, sole, salmon and sturgeon, along with its red caviar (fish eggs), smelt, cod, seal and otter. Its rocky coves and beaches produced clams, and crabs, succulent mussels, and barnacles. They also hunted all sorts of waterfowl, such as ducks, geese and gulls. This sea was a garden also that produced a year-round crop of kelp and seaweed. They used the salt water as a kind of bouillon for their soups, stews and vegetables. When it came to the fruit of the land they used camass toots, wild carrots, potatoes, acorns, hazelnuts, wild salad greens, huckleberries, blackberries, raspberries, wild strawberries, and salmonberries.

EVERY LITTLE THING
IS SENT FOR SOMETHING,
AND IN THAT THING
THERE SHOULD BE HAPPINESS,
AND THE POWER TO MAKE HAPPY.
LIKE THE GRASSES
SHOWING TENDER FACES TO EACH OTHER,
THIS WE SHOUD DO.

—Black Elk
Black Elk Speaks

FOODS OF AMERICAN INDIANS

Wild Berries

Blackberries	Hackberries
Cranberries	Strawberries
Gooseberries	Haws-red black
Elderberries	yellow
Raspberries	Huckleberries

Wild Fruit

Cherries	Grapes
Plums	Pawpaws
Currents	Maple sugar
Persimmons	Crabapples

Fish

Abalone	Clams
Mussels	Crayfish
Eel	Crabs
Oysters	Turtles

Vegetables

Artichokes
Sunflower seeds
Wild Rice
Mushrooms
Pumpkins
Beans

Tomatoes
Maize (corn)
Melons
Potatoes
Squash
Pig Weed seed

Fowl

Wild Ducks
Quail
Partridge
Pigeon (Dove)

Wild Turkey
Goose
Pheasant

Meats

Alligator
Moose
Bear
Beavers
Buffalo
Caribou
Deer
Elk

Antelope
Rabbits
Jack Rabbits
Goats
Squirrels
Racoon
Opossum
Muskrats

Nuts

Acorn
Beechnuts
Walnuts
Hickory nuts
Pecans
Butternuts

Peanuts
Pinon nuts
Coffee
Hazel nuts
Chestnuts

Flowers

Mayapple
Violet Leaves
Honey Locust seed
Wildcrab apple
Sumac Berry

Solomon's seal
Trilium
Primrose seed
Cattails
Adders tongue

Leaves

Beach

Water Cress

LEGEND OF CORN (MAIZE)

Many years ago the great Kahkawkonty told how the Great Spirit Appeared to a wise forefather and showed him the plant, *Corn*. The Great Spirit *told him to preserve two ears on the plant until the next Spring; then plant the kernels. He should preserve the whole crop and Send two ears to each of the surrounding nations, with the injunction that They were not to eat any of it until their third crop. The wise Indian did as He was commanded. By this means the corn was distributed among all Native American Indians.*

All plants are our brothers and sisters. They talk to us and if we listen, we can hear them. Tell me and I'll forget. Show me, and I may not remember. Involve me, and I'll understand ... Before eating, always take time to thank the food. When we show our respect for other living things, they respond with respect for us. Most of us do not look as handsome to others as we do to ourselves. Those that lie down with dogs, get up with fleas. We always return to our first loves.—

The Native Nations Museum wanted to preserve these recipes as a permanent tribute to all the Nations of the American native people and share the culture with all people wherever they may live. Thank the Grandfather and the Lord of Harvest.
For the first inhabitants of this continent, the Native Americans, nature was their pharmacy and grocery store. They were on a first name basis with hundreds of plants, grasses, herbs and animals.

BREADS

Fry Bread

4 cups white flour
1/2 teaspoon salt
1 tablespoon baking powder

    Combine all ingredients. Add about 1 ½ cups lukewarm water and knead until dough is soft but not sticky. Shape dough into balls the size of a small peach. Shape into patties by hand; dough should be about 1/2 inch thick.
    Make a small hole in the center of the round.
    Fry one at a time in about 1 inch of hot lard or shortening in a heavy pan. Brown on both sides. Drain on paper towels and serve hot with honey or jam.

NAVAJO FRY BREAD

1 Cup flour
1 t baking powder
1/4 C powdered milk
1/4 t salt
warm water

    Combine the ingredients and slowly add enough warm water to form dough. On a lightly floured surface, knead dough until it is smooth soft and not sticky. Cover and let rest one hour.
    Shape into small balls and pat into flat circles about
1/4-1/2 inch thick. Set aside.

In skillet, heat 1/2 inch vegetable oil. Brown dough circles on each side and drain on paper towels.

Serve with chile beans and your favorite taco toppings for "Navajo Tacos."

Navajo Fry Bread (2)

Serving Size : 4
1 cup white flour
1/2 cup whole wheat flour
1 tablespoon sugar
1/2 teaspoon baking powder
1/4 teaspoon salt
1/2 cup honey
vegetable oil

Mix dry ingredients. Add water to dry ingredients, mix well. Knead dough on a floured board till it becomes elastic. Let dough rest 10 minutes, covered. Roll out dough till it is 1/2 inch thick. Cut into squares or circles. Deep-fry at 370F till golden brown; drain on paper towels.

Drizzle with honey and serve.

Pumpkin Muffins

1 cup raisins
1/2 cup unsweetened orange juice
1/2 cup egg substitute
1 cup canned pumpkin
1/2 cup sugar
1/2 tsp. ground cloves
1 tsp. ground cinnamon

1/2 tsp. salt
1/3 cup canola oil
1 cup all-purpose flour
3/4 cup whole wheat flour
1 1/2 tsp. baking powder
1/2 tsp. baking soda

Soak raising in orange juice for 5 minutes. Do not drain.

In large mixing bowl, stir in pumpkin, egg substitute, sugar, cloves, cinnamon and salt. Add oil, mix well. Stir together flours, baking powder and baking soda. Add to pumpkin mixture with the raisin-orange juice mixture and stir to mix. Fill paper-lined muffin cups 2/3 full. Bake at 400F for about 25 minutes. Remove from muffin tins and cool on wire rack.

Easy Molasses Bread

This bread is made by the quick one-rise method, which does not require any kneading. Adding blackstrap molasses appears to give it a slight sweetness and also makes it more nutritious. Suitable for freezing.

Makes 3 large (2-pound) loaves
butter or pure vegetable margarine
13 cups whole wheat flour
1 slightly heaping tablespoon salt
2 packets instant yeast
1 slightly heaping tablespoon molasses

Grease three large bread pans—or the equivalent, including cake pans, if you wish—generously with butter or margarine. Tip the flour and salt into a large bowl and add the yeast. Mix gently. Dissolve the molasses in a little tepid water taken from 6 1/4 cups. Add this to the flour, then mix in the rest of the water, going carefully at the end in case you don't need quite all of it. The finished mixture needs to be too wet to leave the sides of the bowl clean; it should feel 'slippery' but not completely sloppy. Half fill the pans with the mixture; cover them with plastic wrap or a damp dish towel, and leave to rise. Meanwhile set the oven to 400°F. When the loaves have risen to within 1/2 inch of the tops of the pans, put them in the oven. Bake large loaves for 45 minutes, and small ones for about 35 minutes, or until they are brown and firm to the touch, and sound hollow when you slip them out of the pans and tap them on the base with your knuckles. If you wish, you can crisp the base and sides a bit more by putting the loaves back into the oven for a few minutes after you've taken them out of the pans. Cool the bread on a wire rack.

Blueberry Muffins

1 cup oats
1 cup buttermilk
1 cup white wheat flour
1 teaspoon baking powder
1/2 teaspoon baking soda
1/2 teaspoon salt
3/4 cup brown sugar
1 egg
1/4 cup butter—melted

1 cup fresh blueberries—drained well—or—1 cup frozen blueberries—thawed, drained Preheat oven to 400°F. Combine oats and buttermilk in a small bowl; set aside and let stand. Combine flour, baking powder, soda, salt, brown sugar, stir well. Add egg and butter to oats. Add dry ingredients and stir just until

all is moistened. Fold in blueberries. Spoon into muffin pan until three-quarters full each. Bake for 17 to 20 minutes

Blueberry Popover

1 cup milk or soymilk
1/2 teaspoon vanilla extract
2 tablespoons butter—melted
1/4 teaspoon salt
1/8 teaspoon fresh ground nutmeg
1/4 cup granulated sugar
1 cup sifted white flour
2 eggs, beaten
1/4 teaspoon ground cinnamon
1 cup blueberries or other berries

Mix first 5 ingredients plus 3 tablespoon sugar in a large bowl. Stir in flour, and then eggs until just combined; let this batter stand for 5 minutes. Meanwhile, mix remaining 1 tablespoon sugar and cinnamon in a separate bowl; set aside.

Adjust oven rack to middle position and heat oven to 450°F. Place berries in a buttered 9-inch pie pan. Pour batter over the berries; sprinkle cinnamon-sugar over the batter. Transfer pan to the oven and bake for 20 minutes. Reduce oven temperature to 350°F; bake until popover is firm and golden brown, 15 to 20 minutes longer. Cut popover into wedges and serve immediately.

Blue Corn Scones

1/2 cup Blue Corn Meal
1 3/4 cup all-purpose flour
1/3 teaspoon baking powder

1/4 teaspoon salt
1/4 lb. chilled butter
1/4 cup light brown sugar
1 egg
1/2 milk
1/2 teaspoon vanilla extract

Preheat oven to 375 degrees F.
Grease & flour a baking sheet
Stir the dry ingredients in a bowl then cut the butter into the dry mixture with a pastry blender (or suitable substitute) to form a course meal. Beat the egg with the milk, sugar, and vanilla. When smooth, stir into the other mixture until the dough holds together. Knead briefly on a floured surface; pat into an 8" circle; place on baking sheet. Using a pizza cutter or serrated knife, score circle into 8 wedges. Bake for 15 or 20 minutes

Blue Corn Flapjacks

Two eggs
1 1/2 cups milk
1 tablespoon butter
3/4 cup all-purpose flour
3/4 cup blue roasted cornmeal
1 1/2 teaspoons baking soda
2 tablespoons sugar
1 teaspoon salt

Mix all ingredients in a blender. Let stand for 5 minutes. Do not re-mix or stir. Pour serving sized amounts from blender to lightly oiled grill. Wait until bubbles form on top of flapjack then flip artfully with a great flourish and considerable bravado. Remove from grill when second side is cooked. Serve topped with a pat of butter and syrup, marmalade, applesauce, or whatever.

Blue Corn Flour Tortillas (Modern Style)

1/3 cup sifted all-purpose flour
1 cup water
1 2/3 cups blue cornmeal

Combine flour and cornmeal in bowl. Stir in water and make dough.
Shape into twelve balls and roll each between two sheets greased wax paper. (Or pat between palms the old style).
Cook in a slightly greased griddle with medium heat until lightly brown on both sides.

Wild Sage Bread

1 package dry yeast
1 cup cottage cheese
1 egg
1 tablespoon melted shortening
1 tablespoon sugar
2 teaspoons crushed dried sage
1/2 teaspoon salt
1/4 teaspoon baking soda
2 1/2 cups flour

Combine sugar, sage, salt, baking soda and flour. Dissolve yeast in 1/4 cup warm water. Beat egg and cottage cheese together until smooth. Add melted shortening and yeast. Add flour mixture slowly to egg mixture, beating well after each addition until a stiff dough is formed. Cover dough with cloth and put in warm place until double in bulk (about 1 hour). Punch dough down, knead for one minute and place in well-greased pan. Cover and let rise for 40 minutes. Bake in a 350-degree oven for 50 minutes. Brush top with melted shortening and sprinkle with crushed, roasted pine nuts or coarse salt.

Salt Rising Bread

1 cup milk
1 teaspoon salt
2 tablespoons cornmeal
2 tablespoons sugar

   2nd sponge:
1 cup lukewarm water
   Pinch salt
1 tablespoon sugar
2 cups sifted flour
2 tablespoons shorting

Dough

2 1/4 cups shifted flour

Scald milk, cool, add cornmeal, salt, sugar. Pour into bowl, cover, put into a warm place. Let stand 6 hours or so until bubbles cover dough. Then add second sponge. Mix again. Cover and place into a pan of warm water (120 degrees). Let stand until light. Than add remaining flour until stiff enough to knead. Knead for 15 minutes. Shape into loaves. Place in a greased pan. Brush tops with melted butter or shortening. Cover and let stand until more than doubled in size. Bake at 375 degrees for ten (10) minutes. Lower heat to 350 degrees and bake for 25 to 30 minutes longer.

Bean Bread (Early Settlers)

4 cups cornmeal
2 cups cooked beans
½ teaspoon soda
2 cups boiling water

(Note: soda is used in place of lye water)
Put cornmeal in bowl, mix in drained beans, Hollow out a hole and put in soda and water. Make stiff dough enough to form balls. Drop balls into pot of boiling water. Cook about 45 minutes or until done. Serve with cooked greens and pork.

Ash Bread

2 cups cornmeal
1 cup buttermilk
½ teaspoon soda
1/3 cup fat

(Soda is used where earlier lye water was used)
Enough water to make dough when mixed with above. Add salt to taste.

Old way:

Make a hole in center of the ashes of a hit fire—rake down to the hearth place the dough in the hole. Let it make a crust and cover with hot ashes and embers. Bake to suit taste.

New way:

Place dough into a pan and place uncovered into an oven set at 400 to 450 degrees. Bake the bread for 25 to 30 minutes or until done.

Crackling Bread

2 cups cornbread
2 cups cracklings
1 tablespoon salt

Use enough hot water to make dough thick enough to shape into small loaves. It's better to use crackling with the least fat, and be sure to break it into small pieces. Bake in a moderate oven, 400 to 450 degrees for about 45 minutes, (Crackling is fried pork skins).

Cornbread

1/2 cup whole wheat flour
3/4 cup white flour
3/4 cup polenta or corneal
4 tablespoons sugar
5 teaspoons baking powder
1/2 teaspoon salt
1/3 cup + 2 tablespoons applesauce

1/2 cup low fat soy milk
1/2 cup water

Mix dry ingredients in a bowl. Mix wet ingredients in another bowl. Add wet to dry and stir well. Bake at 375° for about 30 minutes, or until golden brown.

Huckleberry Bread

2 cups Self-rising flour
1 Egg
1 cup Sugar
1 stick butter
1 cup Milk
1 teaspoon Vanilla extract
2 cups Berries (huckleberries or blueberries)

Cream eggs, butter and sugar together. Add flour, milk, and vanilla. Sprinkle flour on berries to prevent them from going to the bottom. Add berries to mixture. Put in baking pan and bake in over at 350 degrees for approximately 40 minutes or until done.

NOTES:

MEATS

FIVE HOUR STEW

1 & ½ lb. Venison
1 cup celery, chopped
6 carrots, sliced
1 onion, sliced
4 medium potatoes, sliced
1 8 oz. can tomatoes or 8 fresh crushed
1 tbsp. Sugar
8 oz beef broth or stock
2 tbsp. Corn starch
2 tsp. Salt
2 16 oz. Tomato juice

Putt all ingredients into a large pot. Mix and cover with tomato juice plus 2 inches. Cover; simmer for 5 hours at 350 F. Stirring the stew occasionally. Serve hot.

VENISON POT ROAST WITH CRANBERRIES

3lb. Venison roast
Flour
2 tbsp. Fat
3 cups boiling water
2 cups cranberries (raw)
½ cup onions, diced
½ cup celery, diced
1 large bay leaf

6 sprigs parsley
2 whole cloves
1 ½ tsp. Salt

Wash and pat meat dry. Sprinkle meat with a little flour and then brown on all sides in heated fat. Add the remaining ingredients except salt. Cover and bring to a boil then simmer for 2 ½ hours. Add salt and turn meat over in gravy. If necessary, thicken gravy before serving. Serves 6.

BUFFALO STEW

2lbs buffalo
¼ cup oil
2 cups dried corn
2 large onions, chopped
2 cloves garlic minced
3 carrots, Sliced
1 tsp. Oregano
2 potatoes, cubed
8 cups water
1 green pepper, sliced
1 tsp. Salt, pepper to taste

Cut buffalo into 1" cubes and brown on oil. Remove to a plate and sauté onions and garlic in meat oil, Return meat to pan and add water and seasoning. Cook 2 hours or until meat is tender. Add remaining vegetables and cook until done, approximately 30 minutes.

FRIED RABBIT

1 to 2 rabbits cut into serving pieces
Milk
Flour
Oil

Dip rabbit in milk then coat with flour. Fry in hot oil until browned. Cover with water and lower heat and simmer covered for 1 & ½ hours until tender.

RABBIT SOUP

Left over rabbit meat and bones
¼ thyme
1 soup bone
1 bay leaf
¼ lb. Salt pork
4 cups chicken broth
3 carrots, quartered
1 cup potatoes, diced
1 onion, quartered
½ cup celery, diced
1 clove garlic
salt and pepper
¼ tsp. Parsley

Remove all meat from bones and set aside. In a kettle combine bones and soup bones and salt pork. Add carrots, onion, garlic, parsley, thyme, and bay leaf. Cover with water and simmer until almost dry. Add chicken broth and simmer 15 minutes. Strain broth and adjust the seasoning to taste. Add potatoes and simmer until tender. Add celery and carrots and cook 20 minutes longer. Add rabbit meat and heat thoroughly and serve.

OPEN FIRE WILD TURKEY

1 turkey, dressed seasoning to taste

Rub salt liberally on inside of turkey. Run stick diagonally through turkey from front of tail to breast bone. Tie tightly to stick. Roast over low fire 3 to 4 hours turning every so often. Near the end of roasting period throw seasonings to burn on the fire for additional flavor.

Chipotle-Glazed Roast Chicken with Sweet Potatoes

Makes: 6 servings
Prep time: 15 minutes
Cook time: 35 minutes

Ingredients

4 sweet potatoes (10 ounces each), peeled and cut into 1-inch pieces
2 1/2 tablespoons olive oil
4 chipotle chilies in adobo sauce, minced
2 garlic cloves, minced
2 tablespoons honey
2 teaspoons cider vinegar
1 1/4 teaspoons salt, plus additional to taste
1 teaspoon cumin
1/2 teaspoon cinnamon
6 boneless, skinless chicken breasts (2 pounds), rinsed and patted dry
Chopped cilantro, for garnish (optional)

Directions:

Preheat the oven to 400 degrees. In a medium bowl, toss the sweet potatoes in the olive oil and scatter on the bottom of a roasting pan. Roast for 15 minutes. 2. In a small bowl, mix together the chilies, garlic, honey, vinegar, salt, cumin, and cinnamon to make a paste. Rub the paste evenly over each breast. 3. Place the chicken breasts on top of the sweet potatoes and roast until the chicken is just cooked through, about 25 to 30 minutes. Serve garnished with cilantro if desired.

VEGETABLES

Succotash

1 lb. bag of (large) Lima beans,
1 16 oz can of Cream Corn
1 (small piece) Salt Pork (optional)
1/2 (small) Onion (cut fine)
2 tablespoons Butter
1/2 cup Sugar
Salt & Pepper (season to taste)

Preparation:

    Wash lima beans and place in a large (5qrt) pot.
    Add water (4 qts), saltpork, butter, sugar, salt & pepper.
    Bring to a boil. Cook till beans are tender.
    Add cream corn and cook additional 5 minutes.
    Remove from heat and enjoy.

Baked Pumpkin

1 small pumpkin, peeled and cut into cubes
1 cup sugar
1 teaspoon salt
Cinnamon

Place pumpkin cubes in a baking dish and sprinkle with sugar and salt. Cover pan with foil and bake in 325-degree oven until soft. Sprinkle with cinnamon.

Fried Hominy

Several Strips of Bacon
2 ½ cups of White Hominy
Onion if desired
Black Pepper to taste

Preparation:

Fry bacon crisp. Remove from pan.
Drain most of grease. Add hominy. Fry hominy
in bacon grease. Crumble bacon & mix in hominy.

Pinto Bean Casserole

1 1/2 cups freshly cooked pinto beans, drained
1/2 cup diced green pepper
2 scallions, minced
1 teaspoon olive oil
2/3 cup diced tomato
1 teaspoon chili powder
1/2 teaspoon dried oregano
1/2 teaspoon ground coriander
1/2 cup egg substitute
1/4 cup (1-2 ounces) reduced fat sharp cheddar cheese

In a large saucepan over medium heat, saute green pepper and minced scallion in olive oil for 5 minutes, or until soft. Stir in the drained pinto beans, tomato, chili powder, oregano and coriander. Cook; stirring constantly for 2 minutes. Remove from heat and stir in the egg substitute. Coat a 2 cup casserole with vegetable cooking spray. Add the bean mixture and spread evenly. Sprinkle with shredded cheese. Bake at 375 F for 20 minutes or until the filling is set.

Meatless Chili

1 cup dried pinto or kidney beans
3 cups water
1 tablespoon vegetable oil
2 cups chopped onion
1 green bell pepper, chopped
2 cups chopped tomatoes
1 6-ounce can no-salt added tomato paste
3/4 cup water
3 tablespoons chili powder
1 tablespoon cider vinegar
2 teaspoons minced garlic
1 teaspoon oregano
1 teaspoon cumin
1/2 teaspoon ground pepper
1 bay leaf

Place beans and 3 cups of water in saucepan. Bring to boil and cook 2 minutes. Do not drain. Set aside for 1 hour, and then return beans to heat, adding water to cover if necessary. Simmer for 1 hour, or until beans are tender. Drain and set aside. Heat oil in a large skillet or stockpot over medium-high heat. Add onion and bell pepper. Cook until onion is translucent. Add beans and remaining ingredients. Bring to a boil. Reduce heat and simmer 1 1/2 hours, stirring occasionally. Remove bay leaf.

Green Beans and Peppers

1 cup low-sodium chicken broth
4 cups fresh whole green beans or 16 oz. package frozen green beans
1 tablespoon margarine
1 medium red pepper cut into strips
¼ teaspoon garlic powder (optional)
salt and pepper to taste (optional)

If using fresh green beans, wash in cold water and snip off the ends. In a medium saucepan bring broth to a boil; add beans and cover. Cook over medium heat for 8 12 minutes. If using frozen beans, time according to package directions. Melt margarine in a small skillet and add the pepper strips. Sprinkle in the garlic powder. Stir and cook until crisp-tender, about 6 minutes. Drain the green beans. In a serving bowl, add the cooked beans and pepper mixture; toss. Season with salt and pepper to taste.

CORN, ZUCCHINI, AND TOMATO PIE

This pie is made from the overflowing bounty of the backyard garden. Fresh corn and zucchini seasoned with dill bake underneath Parmesan-crusted tomatoes to make a scrumptious entrée that can be served warm or at room temperature.

3 cups fresh, or frozen and defrosted corn kernels
5 small zucchini, cut into match stick pieces
2 teaspoons salt
1 teaspoon freshly ground black pepper
1 tablespoon fresh dill weed
2 tablespoons melted butter
3 to 4 vine-ripened tomatoes, cut into 1/2-inch slices

1/2 cup freshly grated Parmesan cheese
1/4 cup dry bread crumbs
2 tablespoons olive oil

Preheat the oven to 375°. In a 13 by 9-inch ovenproof baking dish, combine the corn, zucchini, and 1 teaspoon of salt, 1/2 teaspoon of pepper, the dill, and the melted butter, tossing to coat the vegetables. Cover the vegetables with the tomatoes. Sprinkle with the remaining salt and pepper. In a small bowl, combine the cheese and the bread crumbs. Sprinkle the mixture over the tomatoes and drizzle with the olive oil. Bake the pie for 30 minutes, or until the cheese is bubbling. Remove it from the oven, and let it stand for 5 minutes before serving.

MAPLE MASHED SWEET POTATOE

6 lb sweet potatoes
1 stick (1/2 cup) unsalted butter, melted
1/2 cup heavy cream, warmed
2 tablespoons pure maple syrup
1 teaspoon salt
1/2 teaspoon black pepper
Preheat oven to 400°F.

Prick each potato twice with a fork and bake in a foil-lined shallow baking pan in lower third of oven until very tender, about 1 hour. Remove and cool slightly. Halve potatoes lengthwise and scoop out warm flesh into a large bowl. Mash potatoes with a potato masher or, for a smoother purée, force through a potato ricer. Stir in butter, cream, syrup, salt, and pepper.

WATERCRESS

Gather a large amount; (enough to feed several people) wash thoroughly, Eat raw with salt or wilt with hot grease.

SWEET CORN PUDDIN

10 or 12 ears of corn
2 tablespoons flour
1 ½ tablespoons sugar
1 tablespoon butter
3 eggs
1 quart milk
Salt to taste

Grate corn and mix with milk. Work flour and butter together until creamy, then beat in sugar and egg yolks. Add beaten egg whites. Put into corn and milk mixture and add salt to taste. Place into pan and bake at 350 until mixture has set.

Batter-Fried Dandelion Blossoms

1 tablespoon of water
2 eggs
1/4 cup of nut oil2 quarts freshly picked dandelion blossoms, washed and dried
1 1/2 cups of fine cornmeal

Preparation:

    Add the water to the eggs and bet well.
    Heat the nut oil to sizzle in a cast-iron skillet.

Dip the dandelion blossoms, one at a time, into the egg, and then into cornmeal.

Sauté, turning often, until golden.

Drain on brown paper.

Serve either hot or cold, as snacks, a vegetable side dish, a tasty garnish.

1 1/2 lbs butternut squash
1/4 tsp mace
1/4 tsp allspice
1 tsp ground cardamom
1 tablespoon maple syrup
1/2 tsp salt
2 tsp melted butter

Cut squash in half, scrape out seeds and fiberous strings. Cut into 2" pieces. Steam, which is the preferred method, for 30 minutes. If boiling squash, then cook for 20 minutes or until tender. Cool slightly, and remove the skin from the pieces. Spoon flesh into blender and add remaining ingredients. Process until smooth. Serve with meat or game birds.

Boiled Dry Corn

Six Cups Spring Water Or The Best You Have
2 Cups Dried Sweet Corn
1 Tablespoon Salt

Directions

Boil water add dried sweet corn.
Return to a boil and add salt.

Continue to boil corn and add water as needed to keep water line about one quarter inch above corn.
Cook until tender.
Options to add diced bacon to taste is very good!!

Note: In the early 1800's on our Umatilla Indian reservation we adopted cornhusk into out traditional weaving, using cornhusks, as a result we had a abundance of corn, we removed it from its cob and have continued to dry it from those early days, and it has become a very important and revered food. Especially in its dried form to share with family and friends . . . .

I-Ya (Dried Pumpkin Rings)

Ingredients

Fresh, Whole Pumpkin(S)

Directions

Slice pumpkin into rings about 1/2-inch thick.
Remove seeds. Place slices on a screen or net and place in a sunny spot for 2-3 days or until dried.

Corn Balls (Wahuwapa Wasna)

Ingredients

Tallow or Lard (or substitute water)
Dried Chokecherry or June berry (Saskatoon's)
Ground Dried Corn Kernels

Directions

Grind dried flour corn kernels in a hand grinder.
Grind dried Chokecherry or June berry (Saskatoon's).
Mix the corn and berries together at a ratio of 4 corn to 1 berry.
Put tallow in a frying pan and lightly brown the mixture.
Note: The old timers at this point would put more tallow/lard in the pan.
Dig into the corn mixture with the fingers and an elongated (four fingers wide) mass is formed. That's why they call it in Dakota Aquaplane (corn cob).

Red Clover

Ingredients:

Red Clover blossoms

Directions

Red Clover heads, as the individual blossoms are maturing, have a sweet white part near the stem that can be bitten off for a little bit of sweetness as you are walking along. It would be hard to make a meal of it but it is a welcome bit of sweetness on a warm day.

Jellico (Wild Greens)

Ingredients

Wood sorrel leaves and stems; a handfull for flavoring.
Dandelion, chickory, and pokeweed leave; pick a good mess because they cook down.

1/4 lb. bacon, or fatback

Directions:

Pick the leaves of these plants like you would lettuce.

Wash and cook the leaves down in a pot of water.

When they've cooked down, strain them, add a little water, and the wood sorrel, and let them sit and warm. Take your bacon/fatback (if you use fatback, cut it into thin strips to fry) and fry it in a skillet good and crisp.

Drain off most of the grease (save it for other uses) and take the greens and put them in the hot skillet with the bacon, mixing it well. Serve it up, and eat well!

*** Important Note: Be careful to only pick the young leaves of the pokeweed; the ones not showing any red on the underside of the leaf, as the plant becomes poisonous as it gets big and shows red veins.*

Fried Corn Mush

Ingredients

Oil
Salt
Water
Corn meal

Directions

Boil cornmeal and make a thick mush, like oatmeal. Season with a little salt. We used to eat it this way but when there was some left we'd let it cool over night. Next day, slice the mush into pieces and fry in oil in a pan.

Use the same way you would use frybread.

Note: You can add berries, bits of meat or anything else you like to the mush before it cools. Adds taste.

Floral Green Salad

Ingredients

1 Cup of Cattail Shoots (Young)
Half a Cup Oil
1 Cup of Leeks
Be Sure They Are Not Unrolled (Open)
Wild Garlic
3 Cups Fiddle Head Ferns
2 Cups of Lettuce
Sunflower Seeds

Directions

Pick the fiddle head fern in the spring when they are young, up to 6 inches in height and unopened wash these and then drain. Chop leeks add to the fiddle head. Pick cattails early in the spring also and peel first layer to get to the tender shoots. The roots are also used as well. Wash and chop and then drain. Add to other ingredients. Cut up some lettuce and add to the others. Add sunflower seeds. Then add some oil and salt and pepper, a little wild garlic is the best or regular garlic. Note: Most ingredients are found in the Spring and in marshy areas in the woods. Be sure to wash wild foods. You will get soaked on your search so wear boots.

Squash Blossoms

Ingredients

Flour
Male squash blossoms
Beer
Oil

Directions

Squash vines produce many more male than female blossoms, especially when they first start to bloom. Encourage female blossoms by picking off extra male blossoms. Coat the blossoms with batter and fry in oil either in a skillet or a kettle until browned, but don't overcook. A simple batter can be made by adding fresh (not flat) beer to flour until a medium thin batter is made (so blossoms don't pull apart). You can add pepper or herbs to the batter for flavor.

Succotash N' Nuts

Ingredients

Pinch Of Salt And Pepper
Half Of Green Pepper
1/2 lb. Lima Beans
1/2 lb. Sweet Corn
1 cup of walnuts or pecans

Directions

Chop up green pepper into small pieces
Mix everything together and cook in on stove for 20 to 25 Min, or until done

NOTES:

MEATS

Grilled Tenderloins—VENISON

Wash and trim the tenderloins well. Rub with white pepper, garlic, and salt. Make a sauce of honey and lemon pepper seasoning and marinate the tenderloins. Roll the tenderloins up foil and place it on the back of the grill. Cook slowly at low flame.

Navajo Taco

To make tacos, you will need the following:

**6 Rounds of fry bread
1 T Lard
1 Head of lettuce
3 Tomatoes
1 Onion
1 1/2 lb. Ground lamb or any Ground meat
1/2 lb. Cheddar cheese**

Green chilies Grate cheese. Shred lettuce; chop tomatoes and chilies. Brown lamb in lard. Divide onto 6 fry bread rounds. Top with cheese, lettuce, tomatoes, chilies and onions. Serve with salsa!

Keh Chuuc

Pit roasted venison

although turkeys, peccaries, and even dogs were raised for food by the ancient Maya, wild animals such as deer, duck, armadillo, quail, tapir, monkeys, and iguanas were hunted with bow and arrows, spears, darts, and snares. This recipe calls for venison to be roasted in a large pit, although any one of these types of wild game can be used instead.

Fresh venison

Salt

Early in the morning, dig a deep pit, put rocks in the bottom and build a roaring fire on top. When the fire burns down, put down green branches. Season the venison with salt, then wrap in leaves to keep it clean. Cover with more green branches and cover with earth. Let it cook for an entire day. Dig up and serve.

Pibikutz

(Turkey tamale)

These tamales are traditionally prepared during the festival of Hanal Pixan, which has since become Day of the Dead in the Maya area. The symbolism of "burying" the tamale in a pit and then "resurrecting" it corresponds with the ancient Maya idea of burying the dead before their transition into the afterlife.

4 C turkey broth
6 2/3 C corn masa harina
1/3 C solid turkey fat
6 2/3 C shredded cooked turkey
1 tsp. achiote
Salt, to taste
1 cup tomato
1 large onion
2 sprigs of epazote (parsley is a close substitute)
(optional) habanero chile, to taste

Corn husks

Boil the broth with ½ tsp achiote, a dash of salt, and a little bit of the masa harina for thickening. This will be part of the "kol" that bathes the interior of the tamales.

Mix the corn masa with the turkey fat, salt, and achiote to make a dough. This forms the filling that will cover the shredded turkey meat. Put some of this corn dough on top of a corn husk. Make a hollow in the dough. Layer this hollow with the turkey and bathe with the broth, alternating with onion, tomato, chile, and epazote. Finally, put a covering of corn dough on top. Wrap everything with corn husks, and then bake for an hour and a half at 375 degrees. Or, for the traditional method, bury the pibikutz in a firewood and rock pit, and let cook for 8 hours.

MINCEMEAT AND VENISON

Mincemeat

5 C. chopped cooked venison
2 1/2 C. chopped suet
7 1/2 C. chopped apples

3 C. apple cider or juice
1/2 C. vinegar
3/4 lb. citron
1 C. molasses
5 C. white sugar
2 1/2 C. raisins cut up fine
1 1/2 C. raisins whole
1 1/2 Tbsp. salt
Juice of 2 lemons & 2 oranges
1 Tbsp. mace
2 scant Tbsp. each of: cinnamon
Cloves
Allspice
2 nutmegs grated
1 tsp. almond
2 Tbsp. lemon extract
1 1/2 C. brandy
3 C. liquid in which meat was cooked

Mix ingredients in order given. Let simmer 1 1/2 hours. Add brandy and shavings from lemons & oranges. Bottle or put in a large earthen crock.

Mom's Mincemeat

5 C. ground deer meat
8 C. ground apples
1 C. vinegar
1 C. water
1 C. brown sugar
1 C. molasses
3/4 lb. suet
1T. nutmeg

1T. cinnamon
1T. cloves
1T. instant coffee
1T. vanilla
Salt to taste

Mix together bring to a boil then decrease heat until simmering (2 1/2 hours). Extra ingredients may need to be added according to taste. Frequent tasting is an important part of the process.

Marinade Venison

1 large onion (chopped)
2 large carrots (chopped)
3 whole cloves
1 tsp. your favorite herbs
1/2 tsp. black pepper
4 Tbsp. butter
1 C. cider vinegar (no salt)

Saute vegetables in butter add vinegar & seasonings pour hot over meat. Turn meat every 2 hours for 8 hours.

VENISON SWISS STEAK—(Contemporary)

2 1/2 pounds of venison
1/2 teaspoon salt
1/2 cup flour
A dash of pepper
2 tablespoons butter or margarine
1/2 cup green pepper, chopped
1/2 cup chopped onions

1 1/2 cup water
1 small can tomato paste
1 tablespoon bead molasses

Trim all fat from venison Roll meat in salt, pepper, and flour. In a small skillet brown meat in margarine or butter. Add water, tomato paste, bead molasses, green peppers, and onion. Bring to a simmer, stir frequently. Lower the temp., and let simmer for about 2 hours, stirring occasionally. Serve piping hot with boiled parsley potatoes.

Blue corn posole stew

3 lbs. lamb or pork roast, trimmed of fat and cut into 1 inch cubes
1 large onion, coarsely chopped
2 teaspoons vegetable oil (or render the trimmed fat or saute some bacon)
2-8 cloves garlic, minced
2 cups, chicken stock or equivalent
2 quarts water, enough to cover posole, add more as needed
21 oz. of dry blue corn posole
or 3 cups, each, of yellow or white hominy (maiz blanco)
8 oz. diced mild green chilies
or 2-4 fresh mild, long green chilies, seeded and finely chopped
6-12 juniper berries, mashed (or substitute a crushed bay leaf)
1 Tbsp oregano
salt to taste
1/2 cup chopped parsley or cilantro
lime or lemon wedges

In a 6 to 8 quart (6-8 liter) pan, cook the onion in the oil until soft, stirring often. Add the water, chicken stock, and juniper berries.

Bring to a rolling boil and add the dry posole. Simmer slowly on low heat for 3 to 4 hours. Add more liquid if necessary. Cook the meat as instructed below with the liquids and seasonings, using just enough water to cover the meat. Add the hominy with the parsley and cilantro. Heat to serving temperature. When the posole kernels start to split open, add the meat cubes, garlic, green chilies and oregano and cook on low heat for about 1 hour longer, until the meat is no longer pink in the center. Salt to taste. Add the parsley or cilantro just before serving. Serve with lime or lemon wedges. French style bread and a green salad go well with Posole. The meat can be roasted separately, cubed and added at the last minute for fuller flavor. Posole can be made without meat. Blue corn is the best choice, as it has a firmer texture and more distinctive flavor.

NOTES:

BERRIES

Berries are the delicious and often fragile fruits that grow on vines, bushes, and runners. They have many virtues—they're colorful, easy to prepare, good for you, and so delicious that you can serve them for dessert all by themselves. The only downside is that they're often pricey, since it's a Herculean challenge to get them to market before they spoil. Many don't make it, so check them over carefully for mold before putting them in your shopping cart. Berries don't ripen once they're picked, so the deeply colored ones tend to be the sweetest and most flavorful. When you get them home, store them in the refrigerator and use them as soon as possible. Don't wash them until you're ready to use them, and freeze any that you can't get to right away.

Blueberry *Equivalents:* 1 pint = 3 cups *Notes:* Blueberries are small and sturdy, so they're perfect for tossing into cakes, muffins, cereal bowls, and fruit salads. Like other berries, they also make good preserves and tarts. Select firm, dark berries that have a whitish bloom on them. You can find fresh blueberries in the summer, but frozen blueberries are available year-round and work well in many recipes. They're very perishable, so keep them refrigerated and use them as soon as possible. You can also buy blueberries frozen, dried, or canned. Frozen berries get a little mushy after they're defrosted, but they'll work well in many recipes. *Substitutes:* huckleberry (larger seeds and tarter, otherwise very close substitute) OR juneberry OR red currant OR raisins (in baked goods) OR dates (in baked goods) OR bananas (in baked goods)

Cape gooseberry = Chinese lantern = physalis = golden gooseberry = alkekengi = strawberry tomato = ground cherry = husk tomato = golden berry = golden husk = poha *Notes:* Like its relative the tomatillo, the Cape gooseberry is covered with a papery husk. The fruit inside looks a bit like a yellow cherry, and tastes like a sweet tomato. You can eat Cape gooseberries whole, minus the husk, or use them to make very tasty preserves. They're hard to find in the United States; your best bet is a specialty produce market in the spring. **Substitutes:** tomatillos OR gooseberries OR cherry tomatoes.

Cranberry: These tart berries are traditionally used to makes sauces and garnishes for Thanksgiving and Christmas dinners. It's best to buy them at their peak in October and November, and freeze any that you don't use right away. Substitutes: lingonberry (smaller, better flavor) OR Carissa (especially for jellies) OR rhubarb.

Currant Pronunciation: KER-unt. These berries are too tart for most people to eat out of hand, but they make terrific preserves and garnishes. They come in three colors: red, white, and black. If color is not important to you one can use them interchangeably in most recipes though red and white currants aren't as tart as black. Don't confuse these berries with the dried fruit of the same name that looks like a small raisin. You can sometimes find fresh currants in specialty

produce markets in the summer. If not, frozen currants are a good substitute. Substitutes: gooseberries or raspberries.

Red currant

Notes: With their brilliant coloring, red currants make terrific garnishes. They're also pleasantly tart, and often used to make jellies, syrups, and wine. Fresh ones are available in some markets during the summer, but frozen currants are acceptable substitutes for fresh in many recipes. Substitutes: blueberry or black currant (for preserves) or white currant (for eating raw) or gooseberry (tarter) or cranberry (as a garnish) or blackberries or red currant jelly (for sauces; sweeter than whole fruit).

Elderberry Equivalents: 1 cup = 145 grams Notes: These are too tart for most people to eat out of hand, but they make terrific preserves and wine. Substitutes: black currants or cranberries.

Gooseberry Equivalents: 1 cup = 150 grams Notes: These large, tart berries are in season only in June and July, but canned gooseberries work well in pies and fools. American gooseberries are round and about 1/2 inch in diameter, while European gooseberries are oblong, and about twice the size of American gooseberries. They're very acidic, and so they're great with roasted meats, like goose. The freshest gooseberries are covered with fuzz. Substitutes: rhubarb (excellent in fools) OR kiwi fruit (These are much larger than gooseberries, but they're excellent in fools.) or currants (preferably red currants).

Grapes: Many varieties of grapes are turned into wine, vinegar, jelly, and raisins, but table grapes are for eating out of hand.

They're classified by their color—red, green, and blue—and by whether they have seeds or not. Seedless varieties are popular because they're easy to eat, but often the seeded varieties offer more flavor and better value. Substitutes: kiwi fruit or blueberries (in fruit salad).

Raspberry Notes: It's a real challenge to get these hollow, fragile berries to consumers before they spoil, so you'll have to pay a high price for those that make it. Many don't, so check them carefully for mildew before you buy them. A good alternative is to buy them frozen. Substitutes: loganberry or strawberry or blackberry or boysenberry or dewberry or Carissa (especially for preserves).

Strawberry Notes: Strawberries aren't as fragile as other berries, so they don't need the special handling that makes most berries so expensive. The best time to buy them is in the spring, but you can find them throughout the year, though the price might be higher and the quality lower. Select berries that have fully ripened to a dark red. Substitutes: raspberry or guava (especially for shortcakes).

RECIPE NOTES

- Whenever a recipe calls for oil or grease I recommend that you use Native corn oil or sunflower oil. *Be careful; hot oil causes server burns.*

- Grinding corn, seeds and other dry foods can be done with a grinding stone, mortar and pestle, blender or food processor.

- Dried corn kernels can be hard to find unless you grow and make your own. You can substitute fresh, canned or frozen corn, if necessary, but you will need to use a bit less water in the recipe to compensate for the additional moisture found in the corn.

MEASURMENTS

Tsp., tsp. = teaspoon
Lbs., lb. = pound(s)
qt. = quart(s)
pk. = peck
pt. = pint

Tbsp., tbsp = tablespoon
oz., = ounce
gal. = gallon
bu. = bushel

EQUIVALENT MEASURES

The following equivalent apply to all foods except 'pinch'—dry substances only—and 'peck' (pk) and 'bushel' (bu)—fruits and vegetables . . .

1 pinch = 1/8 tsp or less, 1-1/2 tsp = ½ tbsp, 3 tsp. = 1 tbsp,
¼ cup = 4 tbsp, 1/6 cup = 2 tbsp. + 2 tsp, 1/3 cup = 5 tbsp + 1 tsp,
3/8 cup = 6 tbsp, ½ cup = 8 tbsp, 2/3 cup = 10 tbsp + 2 tsp,
¾ cup = 12 tsp, 1 cup = 16 tbsp, 4 cups = 1 qt. 8 qt = 1 pk
4 pk = 1 bu

LIQUID MEASURES

1 dash = 6 drops 24 drops = ¼ tsp 3 tsp = 1 tbsp 1 tbsp = ½ fluid oz
2 cups = 16 fluid oz (1 pint) 3 tbsp = 1 ½ fluid oz (1 jigger) ½ cup = 4 fluid oz
16 tbsp = 1 cup 1 cup = 8 fluid oz (1/2 pint) 2 pints = 1 qt 4 qt = gal

OVEN TEMPERATURE GUIDE

	GAS	*ELECTRIC*	*MARK*
COOL	1OOC 200F	110C 225F	¼
VERY SLOW	120C 250F	120C 250F	½
SLOW	150C 300F	150C 300F	1-2
MOD SLOW	160C 325F	170C 340F	3
MODERATE	180C 350F	200C 400F	4

MOD HOT	190C 375F	220C 425F	5-6
HOT	200C 400F	230C 450F	6-7
VERY HOT	230C 450F	250C 475F	8-9

The Green Corn festivals take place all over Indian country between May and October. It celebrates the ripening of the first corn of the year. By doing this the Creator is thanked for this corn, as well as for the rain and sun that nurture it. The corn festival is regarded as a time to renew one's spirit and express gratitude for the corn, the staple of life. Maize actually means "live" in many Native American languages. Every portion of the plant is used in some way; the kernels for food, the husks for tamales and dills, the silk for tea and the stalks for fodder.

FOOD HINTS

Add a little sugar or honey to something too salty—works if it isn't too salty. If a stew, add a can of sweet corn, juice and all.

Hubbard squash—fry fast—beats boiling or baking for time.

Indian Tea outdoors—use wintergreen leaves with green tea in an enamel pot.

Blueberry Muffins—coat Blueberries with flour before dropping into batter to keep them from sinking to the bottom.

Late fall squash—bury small squashes in the ashes at the campfire and eat before you go to bed.

If you soak nuts overnight in salted water, meats will come out whole.

If your oven does not brown biscuits evenly, especially in the middle part of the pan—string out the biscuits around the edge of the pan only.

If only a few drops of lemon juice are needed, use an ice pick to make the hole before squeezing. The lemon can be used again. If whole lemons are needed, soak in boiling water for a few minutes to get out more of the juice.

Native Folk Remedies

CATNIP: Tea brewed from the leaves quiets fitful babies.

CEDAR: The inner bark pulverized and mixed with clean lard for deep cuts difficult in healing.

DOGWOOD: Tea brewed from the roots is a general tonic.

DRIED SUNFLOWER LEAVES: Smoked in a clay pipe clears the head when you have a cold.

HOLLY: Tea brewed from the ashes of the leaves is used to cure whooping cough.

JIMSON WEED: Pound leaves into a poultice for bronchial congestion or apply directly to sprains with a bandage to reduce swelling.

MUD, CLAY: Packed moist around sprained ankles, knees or wrist relieves pain and reduces swelling.

Salt: Common table salt used as a gargle for colds or yo clean teeth.

SASSAFRAS: Tea brewed from the roots is used as a yonic for purifying the blood.

WILD GARLIC: Cloves ponded and applied as a poultice with a little cornmeal added to hold it together is used for drawing out infection or bringing boils to a head. Change every 2-3 hours.

Wild Onions: Eaten boiled or raw is a cure for dizzy spells or gall bladder trouble.